THE MIND'S EYEBEAM

by Sam Hurt

Andrews, McMeel & Parker
A Universal Press Syndicate Affiliate
Kansas City • New York

Library of Congress Catalog Card Number: 86-71299

First Printing, July 1986
Second Printing, October 1986

Scott Deschaine provided much appreciated help with his airbrush on the cover.

Thanks to Gordon Gidley for keeping the whole thing rolling.

Troublesome Introductory Remarks

Let me say something loud-and-clear, since the author is prohibited from doing so except when drunk and/or in contract negotiations: *This is brilliant stuff*. It's not brilliant like sonnets and physics — no "Why dost thous" or exponential integers — but brilliant in a plain ol' human way. It speaks in *your* voice, oh Gentle-and-I-Presume-Recreational-Reader. Sam Hurt's work has a quality all its own. It's plain, straightforward, and — in a way — Texan. It's also bizarre, astonishing, and wonderfully ironic.

Sam Hurt has the visual imagination of R. Crumb (he's one of the few practicing lawyers who does). He has Garry Trudeau's gift for sophisticated dialogue and George Ade's eye for sociological detail. Sometimes he shows the playful social conscience of Walt Kelly. His work is weird, wise, and funny. The planet is a better place for it. No wonder his book has been selected for placement in the Library of Congress!

I *like* the characters in Eyebeam a lot. It makes you feel good to see Sally and Eyebeam together. In a way, they're models of modern behavior — smart, humorous, and cynical enough to wisecrack about the clichés of relationships even as they deal with them. They *like* each other. They have *fun*. They *smooch*.

Like many title characters in comic strips, Eyebeam seems a bit more level-headed than his supporting cast. Some Texas sophomore has probably already received a passing grade on an "Eyebeam as Everyman" paper. He *is* generally more responsible than his disheveled, procrastinating roommate Ratliff — sort of the Mickey to Ratliff's Donald, the Bugs to his Daffy, the Sheriff Taylor to his Deputy Fife. On the other hand, Eyebeam can be diabolical in his torture of the Law School Nurd. And there *is* the matter of that Hallucination.

For all their faults and weaknesses, there's something to like in all the residents of this Cartoonland Austin. Ratliff, with his stacks of *Playboys* and debris-strewn room in need of bulldozing, still has the *heart* to be excited by a rare glimpse at his old record collection and long-gone puppy "Rags" when he encounters them time-traveling. The selfish and overbearing Rod and Beth ("Studmuffins" and "Babycakes") are harder to like, but their mutual dependence can be touching. Even jerks need love.

It's part of Sam Hurt's peculiar vision that even monstrous apparitions sprung from the dark recesses of our innermost minds would have easily bruised egos, girlfriend problems, and ambitions to local political office. Hallucinations, robots, extraterrestrials — all come equipped with the usual complement of vanity, pettiness, and delusion. In the world of Eyebeam, meteorites, death rays, and overlapping dimensions mingle comfortably with Fruit Loops, refrigerator magnets, and vodka-and-Gatorade blasts. It's silly. And it's something of a relief to discover it's a goofily human universe after all.

Thanks, and enjoy yourself!

STEVE O'DONNELL
— New York, 1986
O'Donnell is a member of the National Geographic Society, and has been head writer for David Letterman since 1983.

7

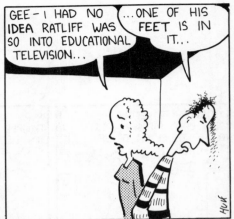

8

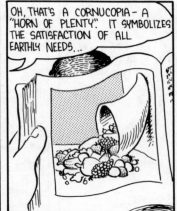

9

Another hazard of greasy hair.

EYEBEAM, WHY DO YOU THINK WE'VE BEEN TOGETHER FOR SO LONG? -BECAUSE WE SHARE THE SAME TASTES AND OPINIONS?

THE BOND IS NOT IN OUR HEADS, SALLY, BUT IN OUR HEARTS. WE SHARE FEELINGS, NOT THOUGHTS.

10

..YOU MEAN OUR LIVES ARE CHANNELED DOWN THE SAME PATH BY A UNISON OF FEELINGS?

RIGHT. OUR SOULS FIT TOGETHER LIKE TWO LINES FROM A SHAKESPEAREAN SONNET.

AW...THAT'S SO **ROMANTIC**!

ALSO, WE BOTH HAVE WEIRD HAIR.

12

RATLIFF, SALLY AND I WERE THINKING WE MIGHT TAKE ONE STEP FURTHER TOWARDS A TRADITIONAL LIVING ARRANGEMENT.

WHAT DO YOU MEAN?

WELL, OURS IS A CULTURE WHOSE NATURAL LIFE-CYCLE INVOLVES PAIRING OFF INTO COUPLES, SETTLING DOWN, AND INCURRING LONG TERM DEBTS..

HMM...

...AND DON'T YOU THINK IT'S ABOUT TIME YOU SETTLED DOWN ON YOUR OWN AND BECAME MORE INDEPENDENT? YOU COULD SET UP YOUR OWN BACHELOR PAD...

MAYBE SO...

HEY! WOULD YOU AND SALLY LIKE TO COME WITH ME?

WHY DO I FEEL LIKE I'M SHOOTING A FAITHFUL OLD DOG?

SALLY- I'VE BEEN THINKING ABOUT WHAT EYEBEAM SAID..... AND IT IS TIME I HEADED OUT ON MY OWN. YOU TWO DESERVE SOME PRIVACY...

YOU ALSO DESERVE A DWELLABLE HABITAT- AND IT'S TIME I CONFRONTED MY HOUSEKEEPING PROBLEM HEAD ON FACE TO FACE ONE ON ONE. - SO, I'M OFF TO LOOK AT RENT HOUSES. SO LONG...

THERE HE GOES- THE LAST OF A DYING BREED.

A TRULY NOBLE SLOB.

YUP- THIS MUST BE THE BLOCK THAT HAS A PLACE FOR RENT...

HEY!...AND IT LOOKS LIKE A NICE AREA, TOO! I CAN'T BELIEVE IT, BECAUSE THE RENT IS PRETTY REASONABLE...

LET'S SEE...4512...4514... IT SHOULD BE TWO MORE DOWN... ...AN·TI·CIPA·HAY·SHUN ♪♪

AND.....**BINGO**.

13

14

Panel 1:
WHERE'S RATLIFF? IS HE OUT LOOKING AT RENT-HOUSES AGAIN?

YEAH—YOU KNOW, IT FEELS LIKE HE'S ALREADY MOVED, AND WE HAVE THE PLACE TO OURSELVES...

Panel 2:
WE ARE NOW THE VERY ESSENCE; THE FUNDAMENTAL NUCLEUS OF HUMANITY: A WOMAN AND HER MAN...

WE'VE BOILED OUR LIVING SITUATION RIGHT DOWN TO THE TRADITIONAL BASICS...

Panel 3:
...MORE OR LESS...

...MORE OR LESS...

ARE YOU **SERIOSLY** ASKING ME TO BELIEVE THAT THIS IS **ALL** THE EXTENSION CORD WE HAVE?

15

16

WELL— WILL YOU TAKE A LOOK AT THIS— NOW IS THE TIME WHEN A WEEKEND OF OVER-INDULGENCE TAKES ITS TOLL...

NOW IS THE TIME FOR DEEP REGRETS —NOW IS THE TIME FOR EARNEST AND AVID RESOLUTIONS OF ABSTINENCE...

HEY— WHERE ARE YOU GOING?

NOW IS THE TIME FOR A LITTLE HAIR OF THE DOG...

HEY, EYEBEAM, SALLY— I FINALLY FOUND A PLACE TO STAY!.. —AND GUESS WHAT? IT'S RIGHT NEXT DOOR!

THAT'S GREAT, RATLIFF!—NOW WE'LL BE NEIGHBORS!

ALSO, YOU WON'T HAVE TO MOVE VERY FAR...

HEY, THAT'S RIGHT!...I WON'T HAVE TO MOVE VERY FAR. —I'LL BE MAKING VERY SHORT TRIPS...

...ABOUT THREE HUNDRED THOUSAND OF THEM...

17

WHAT HAPPENED TO YOUR OLD ROOMMATE AND HER BOYFRIEND?

BETH AND ROD ARE STILL AROUND. WE JUST HAVEN'T RUN INTO THEM FOR A WHILE...

WHAT A PAIR! HE'S SO FULL OF HIMSELF HE ALMOST BRIMS OVER WITH HIS OWN BY-PRODUCT.

...AND SHE'S THE ONLY ONE MORE IN LOVE WITH HIM THAN HE IS WITH HIMSELF.

WHAT DO YOU SUPPOSE THEY'RE DOING NOW?

HE'S PROBABLY GIVING HER THE DEFINITIVE LAST WORD ON SOME TROUBLESOME ISSUE THE EXPERTS HAVE BEEN WRESTLING WITH FOR DECADES.

...SO ALL THAT RUCKUS IN THE MIDDLE EAST WOULD BOIL OVER IF ONLY THOSE FOOLS WOULD SET UP A GOOD INTRAMURAL SPORTS PROGRAM.

OH, ROD-YOU ALMOST BRIM OVER WITH WISDOM!

YES, INTERNATIONAL AFFAIRS IS ONE OF MY MANY AREAS OF EXPERTISE...

YOU CAN DO SO MANY THINGS, ROD.

I GUESS THAT'S TRUE. I'M AWFULLY GOOD WITH MY HANDS, TOO.

YOU CAN MAKE THINGS, AND THEN FIX THEM WHEN THEY DON'T WORK.

EL VELVITO

YES- I'M ALSO A NATURAL AT ANY SPORT INTENDED FOR MALES.

PLUS, YOU'RE AN EFFECTIVE SPEAKER AND A BIT OF A PHILOSOPHER. YOU DO A LITTLE OF EVERYTHING! -AND IN YOUR OWN DISTINCT, MANLY STYLE.

YOU MIGHT EVEN SAY I'M A "JOCK OF ALL TRADES"...

LOW WORDPLAY THRESHOLD.

19

THE AMAZING ADVENTURES OF

RATLIFF

SPACE HERO...

...AS HE DOES BATTLE WITH HIS ENEMY, DR. FORMICA- AN EVIL BAD GUY WHO WANTS TO FLUSH THE WHOLE UNIVERSE DOWN A BLACK HOLE!

20

AS WE OPEN TODAY'S ADVENTURE, RATLIFF VIGILANTLY MONITORS HIS ION BOMBARDMENT TUBE...

I'VE SEEN **BETTER** RECEPTION...

BUT SUDDENLY, DR. FORMICA'S SINISTER RAY ZAPS RATLIFF'S SPACE SHIP...

HEY!

...AND INSTANTLY TRANSPORTS OUR HERO TO A DISTANT ARM OF THE GALAXY WHERE HE IS COMPLETELY POWERLESS...

DAMN!

Sam Hurt

21

Panel 1:
WHO DO YOU THINK IS THE BEST MUSICAL GROUP OF ALL TIME?

GOLDEN MOLDIES
EASY LISTENIN'
BEATLES
MUSAK

Panel 2:

I DON'T KNOW. EITHER "BLOODSTOMP" OR "THE DEATHNOTES"...

WELL, BOTH ARE GIFTED MUSICALLY, BUT NEITHER HAS PIONEERED ANY TRULY SUGGESTIVE GUITAR GESTURES... WHAT ABOUT "SQUISH"?

REAL ROCK

Panel 3:

NAW—TOO POP. LET'S SEE...THE "PISTOL WHIPS" CAN SPIT UP MORE BLOOD THAN ANY OTHER GROUP...

YES, BUT THEIR LYRICS CAN BE SO CONTRIVED... LET'S SEE...

PUBESCENT ROCK!!

DEMONIC ROCK

Panel 4:

AH! **THIS** IS THE GROUP! ....THEY TRANSCEND MUSICAL PIGEONHOLING.

PLUS, THEY WEAR EYE-MAKEUP AND LIFT WEIGHTS!

KIDS ARE SO YOUNG THESE DAYS...

STYX

DIET

22

ROD! - WHAT ARE YOU DOING HERE?

SALLY, LET ME TELL YOU A LITTLE SOMETHING ABOUT YOUR GENDER...

OH, GOD NO!

YOU FEMALES ARE ALWAYS ASKING QUESTIONS, BUT YOU'RE NOT CAPABLE OF **REALLY LISTENING** TO THE ANSWERS...

WHERE DOES HE GET HIS **COLOSSAL NERVE?**

NOW THERE'S A PERFECT EXAMPLE. I COULD ANSWER THAT QUESTION, AND YOU COULD LEARN A LOT FROM MY ANSWER, BUT I-

DID YOU NOTICE ROD IN THE DEN? WHAT'S HE DOING IN THERE?

AT THE MOMENT, I BELIEVE HE'S ENLIGHTENING THE FURNITURE.

BETH, I'VE BEEN FEELING THIS OVERWHELMING NEED TO **MAKE** SOMETHING OF MYSELF...

WHAT ARE YOU TALKING ABOUT, SNUGGLEMUFFINS?

WHY, **MONEY,** OF COURSE.

BUT, ROD, YOU ALREADY HAVE GOBS... YOU GET IT FROM YOUR DAD...

YES, BUT I NEED TO EARN IT FOR MYSELF IN ORDER TO ACHIEVE TRUE MANHOOD...

OOO... LET ME TOUCH THIS HAND- I CAN ACTUALLY FEEL THE TESTOSTERONE PULSING THROUGH IT...

BESIDES, I'M **TIRED** OF HAVING TO BEG AND SCRAPE FOR EVERY GRAND...

IT'S JUST NOT **FAIR!** DOESN'T HE REALIZE YOU HAVE YOUR PRIDE?

23

24

25

GETTING TO WORK A LITTLE LATE TODAY, EYEBEAM.

YOU KNOW, VERNON, SOMETIMES I WONDER IF I'M CUT OUT FOR THIS NINE TO FIVE STUFF...

I CAN RELATE, BUT I SUSPECT THAT WE **NEED** THE STRUCTURED SCHEDULE TO GET ANYTHING DONE.

ARE YOU KIDDING? I'D BE **MUCH** MORE PRODUCTIVE IF I COULD SET MY OWN HOURS...

...I'D TUNE INTO MY NATURAL ENERGY CYCLES, AND WORK DURING THOSE PERIODS WHEN I FELT THE MOST PRODUCTIVE, RESTING IN BETWEEN FOR OPTIMUM PEAK ALERTNESS.

JUST AS AN EXAMPLE, WHERE WOULD YOU BE RIGHT NOW?

IN BED WATCHING TV. - BUT PURELY FOR THE SAKE OF MAXIMUM OVERALL EFFICIENCY...

26

27

WILL THE DEFENDANT PLEASE RISE?

JONATHON CLARENCE DOE, YOU STAND ACCUSED OF MEDIOCRITY IN THE SECOND DEGREE; ASSORTED COUNTS OF ATTEMPTED GOING WITH THE FLOW;...

COMMITTING A CLASS 'C' FAILURE TO TAKE A STAND OR TO ROCK THE BOAT; AND AN UNLAWFUL TAKING OF THE EASY WAY OUT. HOW DO YOU PLEAD?

YOUR HONOR, I'M GOING TO MAKE WHATEVER PLEA YOU THINK WOULD BE MOST APPROPRIATE...

I FIND THE DEFENDANT WIMPY AS CHARGED...

RAP RAP

MR. SNUFF! THERE YOU ARE! I WANT TO ASK YOU ABOUT—

WALK WITH ME, MOLENE. I'M GOING TO EXPLAIN SOMETHING.

MY TIME IS BILLED OUT AT $250 PER HOUR. THAT MAKES EVERY MINUTE—NO, EVERY **SECOND**—CRUCIAL IN THE EXTREME...

CONSEQUENTLY, I CAN'T AFFORD TO DROP EVERYTHING EACH TIME ONE OF MY ASSOCIATES HAS A QUESTION. NOW, IF YOU'LL EXCUSE ME...

SPEAKING OF CRUCIAL MOMENTS, HE'S ALREADY SQUANDERED ABOUT FIFTY **BUCKS** IN THERE'.

HUH?

GENTLEMEN

28

29

MAN!...I'M SURE GLAD **THAT** WORKDAY IS OVER...

NOW, FOR A NICE, COLD BREW AND-... **WAIT A MINUTE!** THIS ISN'T WHAT I NEED...

...WHAT I NEED IS SOMETHING **STRONG**...SOMETHING THAT TAKES EFFECT **IMMEDIATELY!**...

YEAH!...

HEY, RATLIFF— I SEE YOU'RE ALL SETTLED INTO YOUR NEW PLACE...

YUP...

YOU KNOW, WITH YOUR STUFF SPREAD THROUGH THE WHOLE HOUSE INSTEAD OF ONE ROOM, IT PILES UP TO A LOWER LEVEL...THAT'S NICE!

...EXCEPT YOU'RE FORGETTING ONE CRUCIAL FACTOR...

WHAT?

THE TIDES...

Panel 1: WE'LL BE RIGHT BACK AFTER THE FOLLOWING MESSAGES...

IF WE HURRY, WE COULD GRAB A QUICK—

OPERATION "SNACKMANEUVER"...T-MINUS **NOW**!

Panel 2: NOW, WE ALL KNOW THAT GRAPEFRUIT MAGNETICALLY EVAPORATES FAT—BUT MOST OF US RETCH AT THE VERY THOUGHT OF SUCH A NAUSEATING CITRUS...

CHEESE... CHEESE!

CRACKERS... CRACKERS!

BEER.... BEER!

Panel 3: "BUT EX-LAX HAS ALWAYS BEEN A BUDDY TO MY BOWELS"... "NOW THERE'S SOMETHING BETTER!"

AW, DAD-GUM IT ALL TO HECK, A GUY CAN ONLY TAKE SO MUCH...

Panel 4: BETTER? BETTER THA

MUTE

BELT CLIP, HUH? PRETTY HANDY!

I PREFER TO CALL IT A "HOLSTER"...

CLKK

Panel 5: HEY, EYEBEAM— WHAT DO YOU THINK OF THE MOVIE?

Panel 6: HEY!

CLICK

Panel 7: THESE THINGS GIVE YOU SUCH A FEELING OF POWER...

AREN'T YOU EVEN GOING TO SEE WHAT ELSE IS ON?

HEY! HEY! HEY!

HEY!

HEY!

31

LET'S SEE... ALL I REALLY NEED IS PEANUT BUTTER AND COTTAGE CHEESE...

FAMILY SIZE ★

DUM DUMPLINGS DUM

EXCUSE ME, YOUNG MAN, BUT WHERE IS YOUR PRODUCE DEPARTMENT?

DOWN AT THE END ALONG THE SIDE WALL...

WHY, THANK YOU...

I GUESS SHE THINKS I WORK HERE. THAT WOULD OFFEND SOME PEOPLE, BUT I GET A KICK OUT OF IT.

I GUESS I'M JUST THE TYPE WHO LIKES TO HELP OTHERS...

HEY, SONNY— GO GET ME A NEW CART—THIS ONE DOESN'T ROLL STRAIGHT!

YOU KNOW, I'VE ALWAYS FELT I'D UNDERSTAND WORLD AFFAIRS BETTER IF I HAD AN OVERVIEW OF CIVILIZED HISTORY...

...THEN I REALIZED I HAD LITTLE HOPE OF GRASPING HISTORY WITHOUT SOME NOTION OF BASIC HUMAN PSYCHOLOGY.

OF COURSE, PSYCHOLOGY IS JUST A MANIFESTATION OF UNDERLYING BIOMEDICAL PRINCIPLES, WHICH BRINGS IN CHEMISTRY AND PROBABLY PHYSICS...

PHYSICS

FORTUNATELY, I REALIZED THE ULTIMATE FUTILITY OF IT BEFORE WASTING TOO MUCH TIME...

I'VE NEVER LIED TO YOU, MISS ELLIE...

33

35

YOUR HONOR, BEFORE YOU GIVE US YOUR DECISION, I'D LIKE TO POINT OUT THAT MY CLIENT'S ACTIONS WERE THE RESULT OF MUTUAL MISUNDERSTANDINGS - NOT A HOSTILITY TOWARDS OUR CULTURE...

ALSO, I'D LIKE YOU TO NOTE THE REMARKABLE COMPOSURE HE HAS DISPLAYED IN SPITE OF BEING PHYSICALLY RESTRAINED DURING THESE PROCEEDINGS..

I'M SORRY, COUNSELOR, BUT MY HANDS ARE TIED. I FIND THE DEFENDANT GUILTY OF DISORDERLY CONDUCT...

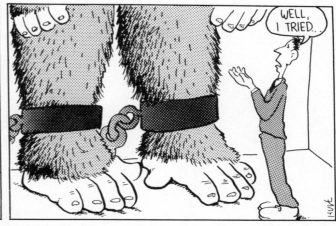

WELL, I TRIED..

BUT WHY CAN'T I HAVE SOME ICE CREAM SANDWICHES?

BECAUSE I SAID SO! BESIDES, I'M ALREADY IN LINE... NOW GO WAIT IN THE CAR...

UNLOCK THE DOOR, PEACHES.

THE ICE CREAM SANDWICHES, UNCLE RATLIFF...

THAT GIRL IS GOING TO BE PRESIDENT SOMEDAY.

EXPRESS LANE 10 ITEMS OR LESS

EYEBEAM- I THOUGHT I HEARD SOMETHING. WOULD YOU GO SEE IF IT'S A PROWLER?

YES DEAR.

NOTICE: THIS STRIP COMPLIES WITH THE 1952 TELEVISION CODE.

I'VE ALWAYS HATED DOING THIS, EVEN THOUGH I'VE NEVER FOUND A BURGLAR...

WHA!

SORRY TO STARTLE YOU, BUT I COULDN'T THINK OF ANY OTHER PLACE TO GET GRAHAM CRACKERS THIS TIME OF NIGHT...

JEEZE, RATLIFF- YOU SCARED THE LIVING HECK OUT OF ME!

YOU DIDN'T REALLY THINK I'D EAT ALL OF THEM, DID YOU?

HI, I'M YOUR GRANDMOTHER. FOLKS USED TO LOVE MY MADE-FROM-SCRATCH MUFFINS. BUT LATELY, EVERYBODY'S BEEN HANKERING AFTER NEW "MUFFIN IN A CAN" ©...GUESS I OUGHTA TRY 'EM...

...SMACK MUNCH... OH, NO! - I DO BELIEVE THEY'VE SNITCHED MY RECIPE...

NO! IT ISN'T **RIGHT**! THIS CAN'T **HAPPEN** IN AMERICA!

I WON'T **LET** IT HAPPEN! I'LL GET A **LAWYER**! - I'LL HIRE THE ACLU! -I'LL...I'LL...I'LL...

...I'LL HAVE TO TRY TO EASE UP A BIT ON MY "WILLING SUSPENSION OF DISBELIEF..."

40

EYEBEAM, I WISH I COULD SIMPLY SIT DOWN AND CHOOSE A CAREER...

YOU'VE NEVER HAD TO MAKE A DECISION WITH SUCH ABSURDLY LONG-TERM CONSEQUENCES.

RIGHT. WHATEVER I DECIDE WILL BE RAMIFICATING ON ME FOR THE REST OF MY LIFE....

ESPECIALLY SINCE WHAT YOU DO BECOMES A PART OF WHAT YOU ARE...

WHAT ABOUT YOU? HOW DID YOU DECIDE YOU WANTED TO GO INTO LAW?

IT SOUNDED LIKE A GOOD PLACE TO SERVE JUSTICE AND MEET GIRLS...

JUST FOR **THAT**, YOU'RE GOING TO HELP ME WORK OFF THAT MEAN OLD INDECISIONAL FRUSTRATION...

SALLY, I DON'T THINK DECIDING WHAT YOU WANT IS GOING TO BE A BIG PROBLEM IN YOUR LIFE...

DON'T FEEL BAD, SALLY- I'M STILL TRYING TO CHOOSE **MY** CAREER.

THE PATH OF LIFE BECOMES A FREEWAY DIVIDING INTO BADLY MARKED EXIT RAMPS. YOU FEEL THAT IF YOU PICK THE WRONG ONE, YOU'LL BE LOST FOREVER...

EACH CHOICE IS A COCOON THAT WILL ENCOMPASS YOUR LIFE AND CHANGE YOUR PERSONALITY.

...AND YOU CAN'T TELL BY LOOKING AT A COCOON EXACTLY WHAT PERSONALITY IT'LL GIVE YOU.

LIFE IS A DARK JUNGLE IN WHICH YOU CAN'T TELL WHAT YOU ARE UNTIL YOU GET THERE.

IT'S AN OBSCURE MAZE WITHOUT AN ESCAPE OR PRIZE TO AIM FOR.. -YOU JUST HAVE TO FIND A NICE PLACE IN THE MAZE..

IT'S A- HEY!

WHERE ARE YOU GOING?

INSIDE. THERE'S A METAPHOR SHOWER OUT HERE!

41

43

A SOLEMN SALUTATION TO THE NEW DAY...

GATHERING MY RESOLVE, I RUB THE COBWEBS OF SLUMBER FROM MY VISUAL INTAKE VALVES...

AS I RE-ASSESS THE ALIEN SURROUNDINGS, MY INSTINCT-LIKE SURVIVAL PROGRAMS LEAD ME TO SCOPE OUT A PRUDENT DIURNAL LOCATION.

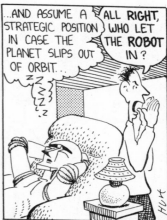

...AND ASSUME A STRATEGIC POSITION IN CASE THE PLANET SLIPS OUT OF ORBIT...

ALL **RIGHT**, WHO LET THE **ROBOT** IN?

HEY, RATLIFF- I THOUGHT WE WERE GOING TO START KEEPING THE ROBOT AT **YOUR** PLACE...

WELL, HE SEEMS TO LIKE IT BETTER OVER **HERE**... DON'T ASK ME WHY...

WELL, MAYBE WE COULD GET HIM INTO A MORE CONSTRUCTIVE MODE...

IT'S WORTH A TRY- WE MIGHT BE ABLE TO PULL A TOM SAWYER ON HIM.

HEY, IM4U- WE'RE GOING TO PLAY A FUN NEW GAME- IT'S CALLED "MOWING THE LAWN".

WE WERE FIGHTING OVER WHO WOULD GO FIRST, SO WE FLIPPED A COIN, AND GUESS WHAT? **YOU** WON!

THIS IS **ONE** PLANET WHERE I COULD DO WITHOUT THE INDIGENOUS LIFE FORMS...

45

ENORMOUS BRAIN, AND STEEL PHYSIQUE-- INTIMIDATE THE SMALL AND MEEK.

-FOR I COULD TURN YOU INTO DUST... - OR MELT YOUR PLANET'S OUTER CRUST...

...OR BRING A NATION TO ITS KNEES! ...AND MAKE THEM ASK ME "PRETTY PLEASE."

BUT STUFF LIKE THAT WILL HAVE TO WAIT; BECAUSE TONIGHT I'VE GOT A DATE.

I WISH YOU'D CALLED. YOU'RE RUNNING LATE!

HI, EYEBEAM. WHERE HAVE YOU BEEN?

OUT GARAGE SAILING...

FROM THE LOOK ON YOUR FACE, I'D SAY YOU FOUND SOMETHING SPECIAL...

YES. A TRIBUTE TO ANOTHER ERA... AN EARMARK OF FINE TASTE... A MEMENTO... A TREASURE...

...A TOASTER.

FROM A DAY WHEN MEN KNEW TO DESIGN HOUSEHOLD APPLIANCES IN A WIND TUNNEL!

47

SO- HOW'S LIFE BEEN TREATING YOU, HANK?

WELL, I'VE SORT OF BEEN TEETERING ON THE BRINK...

BRINK? WHAT BRINK? THIS BRINK?

NO. THE BRINK OF A CAREER MOVE. THE HALLUCINATION BUSINESS IS IN WELL, SORT OF A SLUMP...

DELUSIONS ARE DOWN, FANTASIES ARE ROCKY, AND EVEN THE NORMALLY STABLE REVERIE MARKET IS FEELING THE BITE...

HANK, I'M HAVING A **REAL** HARD TIME PICTURING YOU IN A DESK JOB...

I'D BE OVER-QUALIFIED, WOULDN'T I?

HANK, BY DEFINITION, YOU DON'T EXIST, RIGHT?

NOW, I'M NOT SURE I'M WILLING TO GO ALONG WITH **THAT!**

BUT, THAT'S WHAT DISTINGUISHES AN IMAGINARY BEING, LIKE YOU, FROM A REAL ONE...

YOU'RE USING A CIRCULAR ARGUMENT...

AW, C'MON! STAY WITH ME FOR A MINUTE.- LET ME MAKE MY POINT.

OK, **OK**! JUST FOR THE SAKE OF ARGUMENT, I'LL ACCEPT YOUR HYPOTHESIS...

OH. I KEEP FORGETTING NOT TO DO THAT WITH A STRICT LITERALIST...

49

HANK, HOW DID IT GO WITH THE APPLICATION FOR EXISTENCE?

TAKE A LOOK FOR YOURSELF.

"DEAR MR. HALLUCINATION: WE REGRET TO INFORM YOU THAT YOUR APPLICATION HAS BEEN DENIED. WE HAVE DETERMINED THAT YOU ARE PRESENTLY A SUBJECTIVE EXPERIENCE IN THE MIND OF A HUMAN KNOWN AS 'EYEBEAM'. IN THAT SENSE, YOU ALREADY EXIST, AND ARE THEREFORE INELIGIBLE."

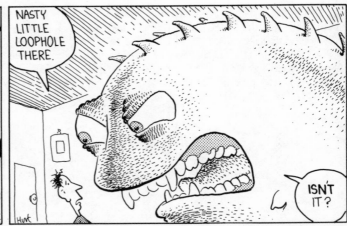

NASTY LITTLE LOOPHOLE THERE.

ISN'T IT?

NOW, SALLY, WE NEED TO LEAVE IN A FEW MINUTES

I'M COMPLETELY READY...

OH. WELL, WE DON'T WANT TO GO QUITE YET I HATE GETTING THERE EARLY

OK, SO, WE'LL JUST KILL A FEW MINUTES FIRST...

I KNOW JUST THE THING...

WHAT ARE YOU DOING? WE DON'T HAVE TIME TO WATCH TV...

WELCOME TO FILLERTELEVISION, THE NETWORK WHERE NOTHING LASTS LONGER THAN THREE MINUTES...

WHAT DO YOU THINK?

HOW DID WE EVER GET ALONG WITHOUT IT?

50

BAD GRAMMAR IS MISTAKENLY THOUGHT TO SIGNIFY A LACK OF INSIGHT BY THOSE WHO LACK INSIGHT.

I HAVE OBSERVED THAT MOST OF US WISH TO BE THOUGHT OF AS "NORMAL"; YET FEW WOULD WELCOME BEING CALLED "AVERAGE"...

THROUGHOUT HISTORY, VALUE HAS BEEN PLACED ON— OH, HI, EYEBEAM.

HI, RATLIFF. DO YOU HAVE A NEW VOCATION?

WELL, I THOUGHT I MIGHT TRY MY HAND AT BEING A FOUNTAINHEAD OF WISDOM.

FORGET IT. ALL BUT THE MOST QUALIFIED ARE DRIVING CABS.

COME ON IN. IT'S UNLOCKED.

DING DONG

MR. STICKY

STICKY PIZZA

BACK THIS WAY...

STICKY

PIZZA

YEAH. JUST BRING IT OVER HERE...

MR. STICKY

STICKY

NOTHING LIKE BREAKFAST IN BED.

AND THAT STUPID HISTORIAN TOLD ME THE APEX OF DECADENCE WAS TOWARDS THE END OF THE ROMAN EMPIRE...

IZZA M

51

52

HANK— HOW WOULD YOU DEFINE A "LONG DISTANCE" RELATIONSHIP?

EASY— THAT'S WHEN YOU'RE TOO FAR APART GEOGRAPHICALLY TO BE SATISFIED, BUT TOO CLOSE TOGETHER EMOTIONALLY TO PURSUE ANY ALTERNATIVES...

THAT'S SOME CATCH, AS THEY SAY...

...I'D LIKE TO MEET THE GUY WHO THOUGHT IT UP... **ZAP**!..SIZZLE...RIGHT IN THE KISSER!...

BUT COULDN'T YOU JUST BE TOGETHER IN YOUR HEARTS, AND CHERISH THE FONDNESS THAT ABSENCE MADE GROW THERE?

WOULD YOU MIND REPEATING THAT?

I SAID, YOU'VE GOT IT ROUGH— NO TWO WAYS ABOUT IT...

...I KNOW. ..·SIGH·...

HUK

BOY, THIS IS REALLY NEAT! UH, I MEAN FASCINATING...

I'D LIKE A **WORD** WITH WHOEVER IS HAVING THIS DREAM...

HEY!

SSSSSSSSHHHT

BLEEP BLEEP BLEEP BLEEP BEE

I THINK I'VE GOT IT FIGURED OUT... THE INTERRUPTION ALWAYS SEEMS TO COME RIGHT WHEN I'M GETTING TO THE GOOD PART... LIFE MUST BE SOME SORT OF COMMERCIAL...

PIZZA

53

PSSSSST.... HEY, RATLIFF, YOUR MID-TERM EXAMS ARE **THIS** WEEK!

WHY DO YOU ALWAYS WAIT UNTIL THE LAST MINUTE TO TELL ME? -DOES IT GIVE YOU SOME SICK PLEASURE?

I'M SORRY, BUT I'VE GROWN TO DEPEND ON THE INCOME I MAKE CHARGING ADMISSION...

TELL 'IM AGAIN!

ON CAMPUS, YOU GET TO WATCH PEOPLE STARTING OUT ON ALL WALKS...

E PLURIBUS UP

...THAT STEEP CLIMB UP THE PYRAMID OF SUCCESS...THE CIRCUITOUS DETOUR THROUGH THE ARTS...THE UNENDING ROUTE FOR THE PURSUIT OF PURE KNOWLEDGE...

...AND, OF COURSE, VARIOUS SHORT CUTS...

ESSAYS...EXAMS... DIPLOMAS...GET THEM WHILE THEY'RE HOT...

CLEARANCE SPECIAL: TWO FOR ONE ON HISTORY EXAM KEYS.

YOU MEAN I CAN JUST BUY AN EXAM INSTEAD OF STUDYING?

THAT'S RIGHT. ONLY BE QUICK ABOUT IT. -I CAN'T HANG AROUND IN ONE PLACE FOR TOO LONG.

NO- I'M TOO YOUNG TO START LOOKING OVER MY SHOULDER.

WELL, YOU'RE A SUCKER, 'CAUSE YOU'LL BE COMPETING AGAINST MY CUSTOMERS...

I'LL BE DOING THAT THE REST OF MY LIFE, SO I MIGHT AS WELL START NOW. BESIDES, I MIGHT RUN FOR PRESIDENT SOMEDAY...

INTEGRITY IS SO DAMN BAD FOR BUSINESS...

BESIDES, I CHEATED ONCE IN HIGHSCHOOL, AND IT GAVE ME FEROCIOUS B.O. ...

YOU THERE- SEE SOMETHING INTERESTING ON YOUR NEIGHBOR'S DESK?...

HUH? OH, NO... UH, WHAT DO YOU MEAN?

I SAW YOUR EYES WANDER TO A NEARBY EXAM BOOKLET...

I GUESS I LOOK AROUND WHILE I'M THINKING... I WASN'T EVEN AWARE WHERE MY EYES WERE POINTED...

WELL, I'D BETTER NOT CATCH YOU AT IT AGAIN...

YES, SIR.

55

YOU WORK HARD ALL DAY...

...SLAMMERIN', HAMMERIN'- GRAPPLIN', SCRAPPLIN'- GOING AFTER THAT SPECIAL GUSTO YOU CALL "LIVING"...

WHAP WHAP

WHAP WHAP WHAM

...AND WHEN THAT SPECIAL MOMENT COMES, YOU HAVE THE WARM SATISFACTION OF KNOWING YOU EARNED IT!

...YOU RELAX, SIT BACK, AND SLAM DOWN A FEW COOL, REFRESHING WOOD GRUBS...

IT JUST DOESN'T GET ANY BETTER THAN THIS!

WHAT IF I WASN'T TAKING A BATH, BUT WAS OUT IN THE MIDDLE OF THE OCEAN?

...FOR ONE THING, I'LL BET I'D WISH I HAD A SWIMSUIT ON...

OOOPS—I BET I'D WISH I HAD A SPEARGUN, TOO. QUICK— WHAT IF I WAS JUST TAKING A BATH?

WHEW!... **BOY**, DO I HAVE A VIVID IMAGINATION!

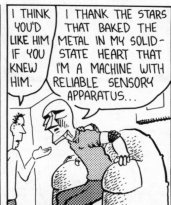

57

RATLIFF, IT'S BEEN MONTHS SINCE YOU MOVED. I THOUGHT YOU'D HAVE YOUR PLACE STRAIGHTENED UP BY NOW...

WELL, I MEANT TO...

...I WANT IT TO BE NEAT AS MUCH AS ANYONE ELSE. I'D LOVE TO FIND MY PILE OF DIRTY SOCKS... I HAVE A FEW MORE I'D LIKE TO ADD...

I KEEP SAYING I'LL DO IT THIS WEEKEND, BUT SOMETHING ALWAYS COMES UP, SO I SAY, "OK- NEXT WEEKEND..."

SO, THE SPIRIT IS WILLING, BUT THE FLESH JUST HASN'T GOTTEN AROUND TO IT YET...

SALLY, YOU OUGHT TO WARN A GUY BEFORE YOU SUM UP HIS WHOLE LIFE IN ONE LINE...

YOU KNOW, I THINK MADONNA IS A GENERIC PERFORMER...

YEAH, BUT SHE'S SO... MMMF!

SHE'S DONE FOR MUSIC WHAT FAST FOOD FRANCHISES DID FOR CUISINE...

WELL, I SURE WOULD LIKE TO- UH, MAKE HER AQUAINTANCE IF YOU FOLLOW MY DRIFT.

...THEY OUGHT TO CALL HER "McDONNA".

THEN I DESERVE A BREAK TODAY!! ...SESAME SEED BUNS AND ALL!

YOU KNOW, RATLIFF, I NEVER NOTICED, BUT YOU SEEM TO HAVE A SEX DRIVE...

IT SO HAPPENS, I COME FROM A LONG LINE OF PROGENERATORS.

58

59

60

OH, YUCKY-POO! SOME BIRDIE WENT GOOEY NUMBER TWOOEY ON YOUR NEW XT5MILLION!

WHERE?

THIS IS ABOUT WHAT I'VE COME TO EXPECT FROM THAT LOW-LIFE ANIMAL KINGDOM!

I THOUGHT I HAD SOME KLEENEX IN AH! - HERE IT IS...

MY BAG

THIS IS THE KIND OF THING THAT HAPPENS WHEN THE CONSERVATION CRAZE GETS OUT OF HAND...

...WISH I HAD MY 12-GAUGE!

AT LEAST NO SERIOUS HARM WAS DONE...

NO, BUT IT SHOWS A PITIFULLY LOW LEVEL OF DEVELOPMENT.

...FOR IT IS IN THE NATURE OF MAN TO ASK SUCH QUESTIONS...

I SENSE INSIDE ME A "SELF"... - A SPIRIT, IF YOU WILL; AN ESSENCE WHICH EXISTS INDEPENDENTLY OF THIS FLESH...

BUT LOGIC COMPELS ME TO ASK WHETHER THAT "SELF" IS MERELY A NEUROLOGICAL BY-PRODUCT OF THE MORTAL MACHINERY WE CALL BRAIN CHEMISTRY...

IN OTHER WORDS, WHAT ARE YOU?

IN OTHER WORDS, WHAT DIFFERENCE DOES IT MAKE IF I MOW THE LAWN?

62

YEAH, I'M STILL SITUATED AT THREE INITIAL CORPORATION.

IS THAT A GOOD PLACE TO WORK?

WELL, T.I.C. IS A BUREAUCRACY DESIGNED TO ENABLE A LARGE GROUP OF PEOPLE TO FUNCTION TOGETHER AS A SINGLE UNIT...

BUT IN REALITY, IT PROMOTES RUTHLESS BACK-STABBING AS EACH INDIVIDUAL TRIES TO DIG, CLAW, AND SCRAPE HIS WAY UPWARD AT THE EXPENSE OF OTHERS...

GEE...WHAT'S IT LIKE TRYING TO FUNCTION IN A SETTING LIKE THAT?

FOR THE FIRST TIME IN MY LIFE, I'M TRULY HAPPY!...

HERE'S MY PHILOSOPHY, EYEBEAM. YOU HAVE TO RUN YOUR LIFE LIKE YOU RUN A BUSINESS.

HOW'S THAT.? ROD?

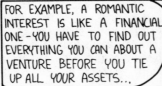

FOR EXAMPLE, A ROMANTIC INTEREST IS LIKE A FINANCIAL ONE—YOU HAVE TO FIND OUT EVERYTHING YOU CAN ABOUT A VENTURE BEFORE YOU TIE UP ALL YOUR ASSETS...

AND IF YOU'RE A CONSERVATIVE INVESTOR WITH AN EYE ON THE UNCERTAINTIES IN THE LONG TERM MARKET, THERE'S ONE OPTION YOU ALWAYS HAVE TO KEEP IN MIND.

WHAT'S THAT?...

...DIVERSIFYING!

63

AH- HOW MY LIFE HAS CHANGED...

TO COME ACROSS A SOLAR SYSTEM. TO COME UP FROM BEING A MERE PRODUCT WHO PROVIDED MENIAL HOUSEHOLD SERVICES... I HAVE TRULY FOUND TRANQUILITY.

UNLESS, OF COURSE, UNKNOWN CIRCUMSTANCES ARE EVEN NOW CONVERGING TO BRING UNDESERVED TURMOIL INTO MY LIFE...

ELSEWHERE, AT THAT VERY MEANWHILE:

RUTHERFORD, OUR MARKET ANALYSIS SHOWS THE PUBLIC WANTS A PRODUCT THAT PROVIDES MENIAL HOUSEHOLD SERVICES...

I'LL FIND IT, SIR.- IF I HAVE TO SEARCH THE WHOLE SOLAR SYSTEM...

"GO FIND A PRODUCT THAT WILL MAKE A NAME FOR THREE INITIAL COMPANY." ~ GEE, WHAT AN ASSIGNMENT TO LAND SO EARLY IN MY CAREER!...

...IF I SUCCEED, IT COULD PUT ME ON TOP OF THE HEAP, PROFESSIONALLY - BUT IF I FAIL, I'M DEAD HISTORY MEAT...

THIS CALLS FOR A SPECIAL KIND OF INSIGHT - AND A SPECIAL KIND OF PLACE TO SEEK SUCH INSIGHT...A PLACE WITH NO DISTRACTIONS...

...A PLACE WITH PLENTY OF FREE BEER AND PLAY-BOY MAGAZINES.

OH. HI, ROD. I'LL GO CHECK THE FRIDGE.

66

RECALLED BY THE MANUFACTURER.. - REALLY DOES WONDERS FOR A GUY'S SELF ESTEEM.

TIC

I MEAN, YOU REPORT TO SOME WHOLLY OWNED SUBSIDIARY YOU'VE NEVER EVEN HEARD OF, AND THEY INSPECT YOU FOR DESIGN FLAWS!..

PLEASE PROCEED THROUGH THE OMINOUS PORTAL INTO THE EERILY GLOWING CORRIDOR..

-WHAT COULD POSSIBLY BE MORE DEGRADING?

HOW ABOUT BEING INSPECTED FOR THE PURPOSE OF BUILDING AND MARKETING A CHEAP IMITATION?

THE FELLOWS UP IN THE UPPER ECHELON ARE JUST GOING TO LOVE THIS!

PRODUCT ANALYZER

WHAT AM I? -A HAPHAZARD COLLECTION OF MATTER, OR A LIVING RECEPTACLE OF IDEAS?

AW, QUIT TRYING TO FIND YOURSELF AND HELP ME LOOK FOR THE BATHROBE DEPARTMENT, IM4U...

JR. APPAREL

MEN'S STUFF

BUT, WHY CAN'T I TRY TO FIND MYSELF?

...BECAUSE YOU'RE IN A DEPARTMENT STORE. -YOU TRY TO FIND YOURSELF ON TOP OF A MOUNTAIN, OR AT A SEMINAR IN A HOTEL CONFERENCE ROOM.

BUT WOULDN'T ONE PLACE BE JUST AS GOOD AS- OH, **NO**!

OKAY...OKAY! I STAND CORRECTED.

TEEN DUDS

APPLIAN[CES]

NEW FROM TIC THE HOME VALET

HE DOES WINDOWS HE WALKS THE DOG! HE IRONS! HE FOLDS!

67

68

EXHIBIT "A"

69

Panel 1: "HOW CAN WE STOP ROD FROM MAKING COPIES OF ME? THE LAWSUIT WAS THROWN OUT OF COURT..."

"...AND WHEN YOU MADE ANDROID COPIES OF HIM, HE DIDN'T MIND A BIT– HE THOUGHT THEY WERE BEAUTIFUL."

Panel 2: "NOW, WHAT ARE WE GOING TO DO WITH ALL THESE?"

"HOLD ON! ...I THINK I'VE GOT AN IDEA!"

Panel 3: "NO! **PLEASE!** YOU **CAN'T** LET THEM GO OUT LIKE THAT! LET'S BE REASONABLE– I'M SURE WE CAN WORK SOMETHING OUT!"

"HI"

Panel 4: "HOW CAN I STOP THIS MARKETING CAMPAIGN? I DON'T HAVE MUCH CLOUT IN THE COMPANY–ESPECIALLY SINCE WITHERSPOON STOLE CREDIT FOR THE WHOLE IDEA..."

"HOME VALET FROM TIC" "YOU NEED ONE!"

Panel 5: "WITHERSPOON! HEY– WHY ARE YOU PACKING UP YOUR DESK?"

"HOME VALET WAS A **FLOP!** –THANKS TO YOUR STUPID IDEA, THE COMPANY LOST A LOT OF MONEY, AND I LOST MY **JOB!**"

Panel 6: "**HA!** WELL, **THAT'LL** TEACH YOU THAT YOU CAN'T LIVE BY TREACHERY AND DECEIT!..."

Panel 7: "...UNLESS, OF COURSE, YOU **REALLY** KNOW WHAT YOU'RE DOING..."

"OKAY– YOU GUYS OWE ME ONE! I HAD TO PUT MY CAREER ON THE LINE TO MAKE THEM SHUT DOWN HOME VALET!"

73

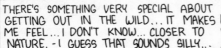

Panel 1: THERE'S SOMETHING VERY SPECIAL ABOUT GETTING OUT IN THE WILD... IT MAKES ME FEEL... I DON'T KNOW... CLOSER TO NATURE. - I GUESS THAT SOUNDS SILLY...

Panel 2: ...BUT AFTER THE HUSTLE BUSTLE OF CITY LIFE, I REALLY CRAVE BEING OUT HERE. I CALL IT "GETTING AWAY FROM IT ALL"...

WHEW!

Panel 3: ...JUST ME AND A FEW CAMERAMEN, AND AN OPPORTUNITY TO TAKE OFF ALL MY CLOTHES...

THE BOOB TUBE WILL NEVER BE THE SAME, THANKS TO THE PLAYBOY CHANNEL...

Panel 4: YOU KNOW, SALLY, EVER SINCE YOU TOLD ME ABOUT "MALE ANSWER SYNDROME," I'VE SEEN IT ALL AROUND ME. WHERE DID THE TERM COME FROM?

A GUY CAME UP WITH IT, I FOUND IT IN THIS OLD COLUMN BY DAVID STANSBURY.

THIRD COAST

Panel 5: IMAGINE - A MALE HAVING THE ASTUTENESS TO DETECT A TRAIT LIKE THAT IN HIS OWN KIND! HOW DOES HE DO IT?

HEY! LET'S CALL HIM AND FIND OUT...

Panel 6: YES, HELLO? I'M ONE OF YOUR READERS, AND I WANTED TO ASK WHERE YOUR INSIGHTS COME FROM...

WELL, BRAIN PATTERNS, LIKE WATER PATTERNS, SOMETIMES ACT IN UNISON TO CREATE WAVES, WHICH THE CONSCIOUS FILTERS INTO IDEAS, WHICH, IN TURN, ARE...

Panel 7: HOW SAD...

...I GUESS THEY'VE ALL GOT IT...

74

THIS WILL BE YOUR NEW HOME, IM4U2... I HOPE YOU LIKE IT. YOUR PREDECESSOR SEEMED TO...

ALL **RIGHT**! MY GOOD OLD EASY-BOY RECLINER!

WAIT A MINUTE! HOW DID YOU KNOW THE PREVIOUS IM4U LIKED THAT CHAIR?

BECAUSE I AM HE. I WAS ABLE TO TRANSFER MY CONSCIOUSNESS INTO THIS NEW BODY...

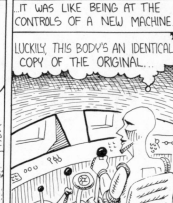

...IT WAS LIKE BEING AT THE CONTROLS OF A NEW MACHINE.

LUCKILY, THIS BODY'S AN IDENTICAL COPY OF THE ORIGINAL...

UNFORTUNATELY, IT WAS IDENTICAL TO THE LAST DETAIL...

HEY! - I WAS SITTING THERE!

UH OH...

APPROACHING END OF HALL, CO-CAPTAIN... SETTING COURSE FOR LEFT TURN.

NO YOU DON'T, CO-CAPTAIN... MANUAL OVERRIDE FOR **RIGHT** TURN.

LOOK- I CAME WITH THIS BODY, AND I KNOW IT NEEDS AN OIL CHANGE. THAT'S BATHROOM, **LEFT** TURN...

WELL, I CAME WITH THE ORIGINAL, AND **I SAY** WE GO TO THE KITCHEN AND PLUG INTO THE UTILITY OUTLET!

OVERBEARING PSYCHIC INTRUDER! ...GAG...

CAFF... CHEAP DOMESTIC IMITATION!

WHAT'S THE DEAL? HE GOT TO THE END OF THE HALL, AND JUST **STOPPED**!

I THINK HE'S BEING HELD UP IN COMMITTEE!

REMEMBER, NO DISINTEGRATION BEAM FOR THESE GUYS - THEY'RE MY PALS...

AW, C'MON - THEY LOOK LIKE SUCH DIPS!

YOU KNOW, SOMEHOW HE SEEMS MORE HUMAN ALL THE TIME - DOES THAT SOUND SILLY?

WELL, HE HAS BEEN ACTING A LITTLE SCHIZO, ALL RIGHT...

EYEBEAM, HAVE YOU EVER READ "SOCIALIZE FOR SUCCESS"? FRANKLY, I FIND IT ALL A BIT CONFUSING...

WHAT'S IT SAY?

A LOT OF OUTRAGEOUS THINGS ABOUT GETTING TO KNOW THE RIGHT PEOPLE, AND OBSERVING THE INTERACTIONS OF CO-WORKERS IN SOCIAL SITUATIONS...

HAVE YOU BEEN ABLE TO DISTILL OUT ANY GENERAL GUIDELINES?

WELL, APPARENTLY, IT'S GOOD TO HAVE A SOCIAL LIFE...

I'D TAKE THAT WITH A GRAIN OF SALT- AFTER ALL, YOU'RE DOING OK...

79

Panel 1:
EYEBEAM, I'VE DECIDED TO THROW A PARTY THIS WEEKEND...

NO! —REALLY? WHAT'S THE OCCASION?

Panel 2:
I'VE STARTED A SUCCESSFUL CAREER IN MOTION. I CAN NOW AFFORD TO SPEND SOME TIME AT BECOMING "ONE OF THE GUYS"...

BUT WHAT WAS WRONG WITH BEING "ONE OF THE NURDS"?

Panel 3:
NOW, WE ALL LIKE TO KID A LOT AROUND HERE, BUT I'D RATHER YOU DIDN'T CALL ME THAT AT THE PARTY. PEOPLE MIGHT THINK I REALLY WAS A NURD!

YOU'RE RIGHT. —THEY CERTAINLY DON'T NEED ME TELLING THEM THAT.

Panel 4:
ANYWAY, I FIGURE THERE'S NO POINT IN STARTING BEFORE SIX OR SO... HECK, WE MIGHT STILL BE RIPPING 'EM UP RIGHT UP UNTIL TEN OR ELEVEN!

LEONARD, YOU ARE A RABID PARTY ANIMAL WITHOUT A LEASH!

Panel 5:
NICE PARTY, LAW NURD —ER... LEONARD.

YUP... YOU CAN JUST CALL ME LEONARD "SOCIAL INTERACTION" NOSTRIL...

Panel 6:
ALMOST EVERYONE FROM THE OFFICE IS HERE —PLUS A FEW PEOPLE I DON'T KNOW.

YES. I WANTED THAT PARTY CHEMISTRY YOU GET WHEN THE ROOM IS FILLED TO THE PERFECT DENSITY.

Panel 7:
FRIENDS OF YOURS FROM OTHER WALKS, I SUPPOSE.

ACTUALLY, I'VE DEVOTED MY POST-ADOLESCENT LIFE EXCLUSIVELY TO MY CAREER AND I DIDN'T KNOW QUITE ENOUGH PEOPLE.

Panel 8:
WAIT A MINUTE! —YOU DIDN'T HIRE PEOPLE TO COME TO YOUR PARTY!?

I REALLY HAD TO SHOP AROUND —YOU'D BE AMAZED WHAT SOME PEOPLE ARE ASKING...

SO. THIS PART OF MY LIFE HAS FINALLY COME.. I HAVE ENTERED GRANDFATHERHOOD...

IT IS INDEED ONE OF THE MOST SIGNIFICANT MILESTONES OF MY LIFE...

IT IS A TIME FOR SELF-ASSESSMENT - A TIME TO ASK MYSELF SOME VERY DIFFICULT QUESTIONS...

LIKE, IS IT TIME FOR THAT LITTLE TOUCH OF GREY AROUND THE TEMPLES?

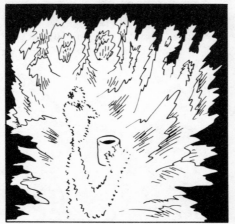

GRANT ME CONSCIOUSNESS, O COFF-O-MAT! .. TO WORK THROUGH MOST OF THE NIGHT REQUIRED PUTTING AWAY RATHER AWESOME QUANTITIES OF JAVA... NOW IT'S GOING TO TAKE ONE MORE CUP TO JUMP-START MY NOGGIN....

FOOMPH

LET HISTORIANS TAKE NOTE THAT THE "HAIR OF THE DOG" PRINCIPLE DOESN'T APPLY WITH COFFEE....

81

WELL, I'M WAITING TO MEET MY FIRST COURT-APPOINTED CLIENT. IT'S PART OF THE SACRED TRUST WE LAWYERS UNDERTAKE...

SINCE WE PROFIT FROM TENDING THE AFFAIRS OF SOCIETY'S UPPER CRUST, WE MUST BALANCE THINGS BY HELPING THOSE WHO HAVE BEEN TRAMPLED INTO ITS LOWEST DEPTHS.

COUNSELOR, MEET "CHARLIE CHAINSAW."

HI THERE, BEAUTIFUL!

...OF COURSE, I'LL HAVE TO CHECK FOR A SCHEDULING CONFLICT.

MOM
STANK
RUM COKE
MODDER

I GUESS WHAT I'M TRYING TO EXPLAIN IS THE CONCEPT OF "PROFESSIONALISM".

YEAH, BUT WHY DO YOU THINK I NEED TO HAVE IT EXPLAINED?

BECAUSE WE'RE IN THE SAME FIRM. THAT MAKES US TEAMMATES. I WANT ALL MY TEAM-MATES TO HAVE JUST THE RIGHT AMOUNT OF "GO GET 'EM".

...SO YOU'RE SAYING I DON'T HAVE ENOUGH!

HONK BEEP

NOT AT ALL! I'M SIMPLY TRYING TO EXPLAIN THAT A PROFESSIONAL IS ONE WHO-

SCREEEEEEEEECH CRASH

I HAVE TO ADMIT, I'VE NEVER SEEN ANYONE BUT A PRO SLIDE FOR A CLOSING ELEVATOR QUITE LIKE THAT...

WHAT DOES IT MEAN WHEN YOU HAVE THE URGE TO BUCKLE UP, BUT YOU'RE NOT IN A CAR?

IT MEANS YOUR GRIP ON REALITY IS GETTING ALL SWEATY...

MR. NESTOR, THIS IS MOLENE. SHE'S BEEN IN OUR ESTATE PLANNING DEPARTMENT FOR SOME TIME NOW. SHE'LL BE WORKING ON YOUR ARRANGEMENTS...

HELLO.

WELL, I'M GLAD TO HEAR SHE'S EXPERIENCED WITH WILLS, BUT IS SHE EQUIPPED TO DEAL WITH THE **TAX** END OF THINGS?

MOLENE, EASE THIS CLIENT'S MIND.

however, section 213 and t ns thereunder as to the incl ross income of amounts a to deductions allowed und 04(a) (3) also applies eceived by an employee f juries or sickness from is maintained exclusive ntributions. Conversel is either the sole co and, or is the so

I DIDN'T UNDERSTAND A WORD. SHE MUST BE A REAL EXPERT.

COME ON, I'LL SHOW YOU THE LIBRARY.

IT FEELS GOOD TO LET IT OUT ONCE IN A WHILE...

83

YOU SPEND THE EARLY PART OF YOUR LIFE LEARNING THE BASIC TENETS OF SOCIAL INTERACTION...

C'MON, MOLENE! -VERNON'S NEVER SEEN IT!

...THEN YOU GO TO COLLEGE, ACQUIRING BACKGROUND INFORMATION AND ENHANCING YOUR CONVERSATIONAL SKILLS...

PLEASE?

THEN YOU PURSUE A CAREER, SO YOU'LL HAVE EVEN MORE TO OFFER- AND WHAT DO THEY WANT FROM YOU...?...

HERE GOES.

OBOY!

...CHEAP THRILLS...

SALLY, YOU REMEMBER IM4U... HE'S A ROBOT FROM ANOTHER PLANET...

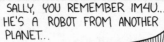

ACTUALLY, THE BODY IS A CHEAP DOMESTIC IMITATION, BUT THE ORIGINAL WAS ABLE TO TRANSFER HIS PERSONALITY INTO THE NEW CHASSIS...

SO NOW TWO PERSONALITIES- THE ORIGINAL AND THE ONE THAT CAME WITH THE IMITATION- SHARE CONTROL.

AHA! I WAS WONDERING WHAT COULD CAUSE A ROBOT TO EXHIBIT WHAT SEEMED TO BE INDECISION...

ARMCHAIR PSYCHIATRISTS. LET'S VAPORIZE THEM...

BETTER HOLD OFF ON THAT... I THINK I MAY BE IN LOVE WITH THE GIRL.

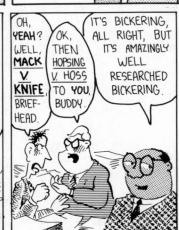

86

I HOPE YOU'RE A GOOD LAWYER I SURE WOULD HATE TO GO TO JAIL!

DON'T WORRY— YOU'LL BE TRIED BY A JURY OF YOUR PEERS... —LOOK.

THANKS— THAT **DOES** MAKE ME FEEL BETTER SOMEHOW...

I'VE NEVER HAD BETTER LUCK WITH JURY SELECTION...

WHAT DO YOU HAVE GOING THIS WEEKEND, IM4U?

WHAT ARE WEEKENDS FOR, RATLIFF? I'M GOING TO PARTY!

PARTY? WHOM ARE YOU GOING TO INVITE?

NO— I DON'T MEAN "PARTY" IN THE OLD-FASHIONED SENSE OF ALLOWING A HERD OF SCAVENGERS TO DEPLETE YOUR RESOURCES.

SIR EEL

...I'M A MODERN GUY. —I MEAN "PARTY" IN THE MODERN, VERB SENSE, "TO PARTY" AS IN "HEY, LET'S PARTY!"

WHAP

...MEANING?

MEANING "LET'S GET FRIED!"

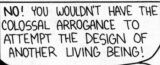

89

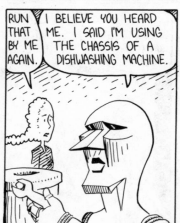

91

MY LOVE IS LIKE A SHINING BULB-
SHE FILLS MY HEART WITH AWE.
A PERFECT FORM BY WHICH I'M LULLED-
UPON HER FACE, NO FLAW.

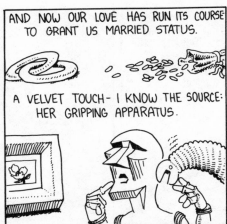

AND NOW OUR LOVE HAS RUN ITS COURSE
TO GRANT US MARRIED STATUS.

A VELVET TOUCH- I KNOW THE SOURCE:
HER GRIPPING APPARATUS.

I ALSO KNOW THE REASON FOR
THIS PASSION WHICH INFECTS,
AND MAKES ME LOVE HER MORE AND MORE:

SHE'S BUILT TO MY OWN SPECS!

BY THE WAY, RATLIFF, HOW'S SCHOOL BEEN GOING?

NO. PLEASE. NOT AGAIN! YOU CAN'T ASK ME TO BELIEVE YOU FORGOT ABOUT GOING TO CLASSES!

THERE'S ALWAYS SO MUCH ELSE GOING ON...

DON'T GET DISCOURAGED. YOU CAN PULL IT OUT AT THE LAST MINUTE...

DO YOU REALLY THINK SO?

OF COURSE! WHAT DO YOU THINK SHORT TERM MEMORY IS FOR?

OH, YEAH! FOR SOME REASON, I ALWAYS SEEM TO FORGET ABOUT THAT!

93

HOW 'BOUT THAT SHORT TERM MEMORY? IT'S A NARROW SHELF, BUT YOU CAN STACK A LOT OF STUFF ON IT, AT LEAST FOR A WHILE...

WEIRD SENSATION, THOUGH. IT'S AS IF THE INFORMATION IS PACKED SO TIGHTLY INTO YOUR HEAD THAT IT'S LIKELY TO **SPRING** OUT AT ANY MOMENT...

YOU DID THAT ON PURPOSE DIDN'T YOU, EYEBEAM?

DON'T WORRY, RATLIFF...WE'LL GET IT ALL BACK IN THERE.

WELL, WE'RE **BACK**—SAY HELLO TO EYEBEAM, SYNTHEA.

HELLO EYEBEAM... ...BEAM.

DID YOU HAVE A NICE TIME?

WE SURE DID! WE—

HELLO TO EYEBEAM. HELLO...HELLO... ...HELLO... ELLO... LLO.. LO...O...O...

OH, **NO**! NOT **AGAIN**!

...OOOO OOOOOOO OOOOO OOOOOO...

IMPRESSIVE! I MYSELF HAVE NEVER BEEN ABLE TO DEVELOP A CONVINCING DIAL TONE.

WOMEN ARE SO... ...SO DARN... **UNRELIABLE**!

...OOOO OOOOOO OOOOO OOO...

THE HONEYMOON'S OVER...

95

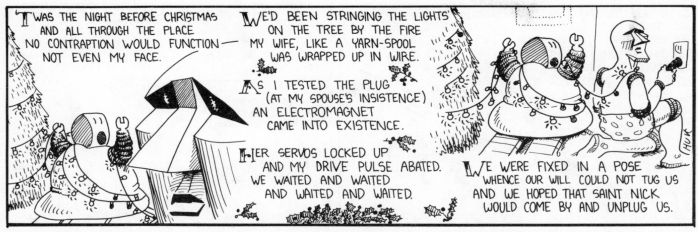

'TWAS THE NIGHT BEFORE CHRISTMAS
AND ALL THROUGH THE PLACE
NO CONTRAPTION WOULD FUNCTION—
NOT EVEN MY FACE.

WE'D BEEN STRINGING THE LIGHTS
ON THE TREE BY THE FIRE
MY WIFE, LIKE A YARN-SPOOL
WAS WRAPPED UP IN WIRE.

AS I TESTED THE PLUG
(AT MY SPOUSE'S INSISTENCE)
AN ELECTROMAGNET
CAME INTO EXISTENCE.

HER SERVOS LOCKED UP
AND MY DRIVE PULSE ABATED.
WE WAITED AND WAITED
AND WAITED AND WAITED.

WE WERE FIXED IN A POSE
WHENCE OUR WILL COULD NOT TUG US
AND WE HOPED THAT SAINT NICK
WOULD COME BY AND UNPLUG US.

A-ONE
AND A-TWO
AND A-

ZRRRRRR

DID YOU GET SOME PICTURES?

WELL, I... UH...

THE GUSTO'S **BACK**!

SUZY OWEN

...SO WE WERE FROZEN LIKE STATUES UNTIL YOU CAME ALONG AND UNPLUGGED MY INADVERTENT ELECTROMAGNET.

IT MUST HAVE GIVEN YOU A STIFF NECK. YOU COULD STAR IN A PAIN RELIEVER AD.

WOULD YOU LIKE A BACK RUB, DEAR?

OH, YES!...MMM... A LITTLE LOWER...**YEAH**! COME OVER HERE AND LET'S DO THIS RIGHT...

YES, DEAR.

MMMM OOOOO... AH.... OH... YOW!... ...

clickity clackity click

HUK

IF YOU'LL EXCUSE ME, I'LL LEAVE YOU TWO TO YOUR OWN DEVICES.

HARK - I AWAKEN. NOT JUST TO THE DAWNING OF A NEW DAY, BUT TO THE BIRTH OF A NEW YEAR!

AND WITH IT, A VIRGINAL HORIZON OF UNTRIED POSSIBILITIES... OF FRESH DREAMS WAITING TO COME TRUE...

AND SINCE I WISELY CHOSE TO FORGO LAST NIGHT'S RITUAL OF ABUSIVE SELF-INDULGENCE, I FACE THIS NEW HORIZON WITH VIGOR AND A CLEAR HEAD...

...AND A HOUSEHOLD FULL OF PEOPLE WHO WOULD MUTILATE ME IF THEY COULD MOVE...

HUK

96

THIS IS SO DARN WEIRD...

WHAT?

WELL, FOR THE LAST FEW DAYS, MY HEAD HAS FELT REMARKABLY SHARP... MY ABILITY TO CONCENTRATE SOMEHOW ENHANCED...

IT'S AS IF MY MIND WAS CLUTTERED WITH STUFFED TOY ANIMALS AND NOW IT'S SUDDENLY REFRESHINGLY CLEAR. WHAT COULD ACCOUNT FOR SUCH A SENSATION?

WELL, THEY'VE BEEN LETTING UP A LITTLE ON THE HOLIDAY MUSIC...

HEY, **THAT'S IT!**

SNAP

...AND TWO GREEN SOCKS REUNITE AND DECIDE TO SPEND THEIR LIVES TOGETHER IN MY TOP DRAWER... **DUNK.**

OKAY— TWO MORE GREYS...TWO WHITES... TWO... HEY— *WAIT A MINUTE*— **THEY ALL CAME OUT EVEN!**

...THIS SHOULD HAPPEN TO EVERYONE JUST ONCE IN THEIR LIVES...

100

MY HANDS ARE ROBOT HANDS - MADE TO PICK ARTIFICIAL FLOWERS...

MY FEET ARE ROBOT FEET - MADE TO STROLL THROUGH METALLIC CLOVER...

MY HEAD IS A ROBOT HEAD - MADE TO THINK ASSEMBLY LINE THOUGHTS.

BUT MY SOUL IS THE SOUL OF A LOVER.

COOL IT, ROMEO. I'M NOT IN THE MOOD...

IT'S SO NICE JOGGING IN THE PARK...

YEAH. TOO BAD EYEBEAM COULDN'T MAKE IT...

WATCH OUT FOR THAT FUNNY TREE...

C'MON, RATLIFF... I'LL RACE YOU...

A SNAG

WHOOPS

RRRRIP

ZOINK

PARK CURB

BOY, THIS IS GETTING TO BE A REGULAR HABIT!

YES- I'D LIKE TO SPEAK WITH YOU ABOUT THAT...

101

Panel 1:
EYEBEAM, MY ONLY PARANOIA IS GETTING SWALLOWED UP BY THE EARTH.

WELL, OSCAR, IF YOU'RE GOING TO LIMIT YOURSELF TO JUST ONE, THAT SEEMS LIKE A GOOD CHOICE...

Panel 2:
WELL, IT PROBABLY SEEMS SILLY, BUT— HEY! WHAT THE—

Panel 3:
GLRG MMMF—

HMM...

Panel 4:
YOU'D THINK A GUY LIKE THAT WOULD WANT TO KEEP TO THE SIDEWALK...

Panel 5:
SYNTHEA AND I HAVE BEEN MARRIED FOR A WHILE NOW, BUT WE HAVE YET TO HEAR THE CLITTER CLATTER OF TINY FEET AROUND THE HOUSE.

I HAVE A THEORY ABOUT THAT, IM4U. YOU SEE, IT TAKES TWO SEPARATE INDIVIDUALS TO PRODUCE OFFSPRING.

Panel 6:
...SINCE YOU PERSONALLY DESIGNED AND CONSTRUCTED SYNTHEA, SHE'S REALLY NOTHING MORE THAN AN EXTENSION OF YOURSELF.

Panel 7:
YOU NEED A **SEPARATE** ENTITY TO REPRODUCE WITH. IN YOUR CASE, I GUESS THAT WOULD BE ANOTHER MACHINE.

UH-OH...

Panel 8:
HEY, EYEBEAM— WHAT'S THE FUNNY BULGE GROWING ON YOUR CAR?

UH-OH.

"UH-OH"?

102

103

HEY, EYEBEAM, WHAT'S BEEN GOING **ON** AROUND HERE LATELY?

FUNNY YOU SHOULD ASK, SALLY. IM4U ACCIDENTLY PROGRAMMED MY CAR TO REPRODUCE. HE'S GOING TO BE A FATHER...

REALLY? OH, WOW. HOW'S HE TAKING IT?

NOT TOO WELL. HE CAN'T FACE UP TO TELLING HIS WIFE, SYNTHEA. AS A RESULT, HE'S BEEN SORT OF... - HOW SHALL I PUT IT?...

... WELL, SELF-DESTRUCTIVE.

EGAD!

I'M MAKING MYSELF INTO SOMETHING EVEN **I** CAN'T SCREW UP— PAPERWEIGHTS!

IM4U, YOU'VE GOT TO PULL YOURSELF TOGETHER...

VERY GOOD. YOU SHOULD GO INTO COMEDY. I'M GOING INTO PAPERWEIGHTS.

LOOK— YOU MADE A MISTAKE. THANKS TO YOU, THERE'S GOING TO BE A NEW FACE AROUND HERE. BUT YOU CAN'T RUN FROM THE PROBLEM - YOU HAVE TO STAY AROUND, TAKE RESPONSIBILITY, AND MAKE THE BEST OF THINGS.

I DO?

IF YOU **DON'T**, I'LL SEE THAT YOUR PARTS ARE MADE INTO A MOBILE AND HUNG IN A DENTIST'S OFFICE...

YOU PLAY DIRTY POOL, SALLY. HAND ME THAT SOCKET WRENCH,...

Panel 1:
OK, SALLY, YOU TALKED ME INTO REASSEMBLING MYSELF. WHAT'S NEXT?

IT'S REALLY **YOUR** BUSINESS, BUT SINCE YOU ASK, HERE'S WHAT I RECOMMEND:

Panel 2:
GO TELL SYNTHEA THAT YOU DON'T DESERVE HER. **DON'T** TELL HER YOU GOT EYEBEAM'S CAR PREGNANT. JUST EXPRESS BITTER SELF-REPROACH...

OK.

Panel 3:
I'LL MOVE THE CAR OVER TO RATLIFF'S PLACE TO AVOID A POSSIBLE SCENE. JUST LAY IT ON THICK, AND KEEP HER IN THE DARK UNTIL I GET BACK TO SUPERVISE.

CHECK.

Panel 4:
...BORN TO MEDDLE.

Panel 5:
YOU MEAN EYEBEAM'S CAR IS GOING TO HAVE IM4U'S **BABY**!?

EXACTLY! HOW DEFTLY YOU PUT IT!

I **TOLD** YOU SHE'D SHOW A REMARKABLY DEFT GRASP OF THE SITUATION.

Panel 6:
BUT, WHO'S GOING TO TAKE CARE OF THE CHILD?

LISTEN TO HER SELFLESS CONCERN FOR ANOTHER. HOW HEART-WARMING.

I EXPECTED NO LESS FROM MY LITTLE JEWEL. IF I CAN STILL CALL HER THAT.

Panel 7:
LISTEN, BUSTER— YOU CAN CALL ME ANYTHING YOU LIKE, BUT THESE EXTRA-CURRICULAR TUNE-UPS ARE GOING TO **STOP**!

NNNG YES, -UNG. DEAR.

SOUNDS LIKE SHE'S GOING TO ADOPT THE BABY.

GOOD. BECAUSE I NEED THE NATURAL MOTHER TO GET TO WORK...

106

107

HMMM...I WONDER WHAT'S COOKING HERE IN EYEBEAM'S KITCHEN?

SMELLS INTERESTING... I'M SURPRISED HE'S TAKING ANY TIME OUT FOR COOKING THESE DAYS...

ESPECIALLY SINCE HE'S BEEN SO BUSY RESEARCHING THE ORIGIN OF ORGANIC MOLECULES.

YOU LIKE THE PRIMORDIAL CHEMICAL SOUP?

109

IT'S LIKE I'M ALWAYS TELLING YOU—THE FREE MARKET SYSTEM IS SUPERIOR BECAUSE IT'S BEST AT ALLOCATING RESOURCES...

BUT THE HEART OF THE SYSTEM ISN'T DISTRIBUTION OF GOODS—IT'S MARKETING! THEY'D JUST AS SOON SELL YOU SOMETHING YOU DON'T NEED AS SOMETHING YOU DO...

LOOK—THIS ISN'T A GOOD TIME TO GET OFF ON THAT OLD DISPUTE AGAIN.

YOU'RE RIGHT...

...WE'LL DISCUSS IT AFTER DINNER...

CHEZ MR. T

THE LOCAL GROCER IS USING SUBLIMINAL TRANSMISSIONS TO DELIVER ITS SALES PITCH.

YOU WILL COME TO "MR. GROCERY" NEXT TIME YOU SHOP. YOU WILL NOT REMEMBER THIS MESSAGE...

WHAT PROMISES TO BE THE BIGGEST BREAKTHROUGH IN MARKETING TECHNOLOGY SINCE THE PAY TOILET SEEMS TO BE WORKING...

R FRIENDS
P AT
ROCERY"

BUT CLOSER INSPECTION REVEALS THAT ONE OF THE NOGGINS BEING INFILTRATED BELONGS TO AN OFF-DUTY ATTORNEY...

STATUTES
CASE LAW
BILLING STRATEGY
LAWSUIT DETECTOR
SEX DRIVE
HADLEY V. BAXENDALE

...AND THE CLEAR BEACON OF JUSTICE STABS ONCE MORE THROUGH THE INKY MUCK OF COMMERCIAL EXPLOITATION.

CLASS ACTION!

A PROMINENT YOUNG ATTORNEY PONDERS ONE OF THE DAY'S BURNING LEGAL QUESTIONS:

HOW DO YOU GET TO BE PARTNER?

...YOU BRING IN IMPORTANT CLIENTS, THAT'S HOW - BUT, WHERE DO YOU GET THEM? -DO YOU JUST HAUL 'EM IN OFF THE STREET?

TORNEYS

BEEP... BEEP
!HONK!
SQUEEL...

HORTBREAD & SNUFF TORNEYS

THERE'S GOTTA BE ANOTHER WAY...

SNUFFLEBUT AND CROCHET
ATTORNEYS AT LAW

THERE'S GOTTA BE ANOTHER WAY...

THERE'S GOTTA BE ANOTHER WAY...

113

WELL, LOOK, IT'S OVER. ANOTHER MONTH BITES THE DUST...

FEB

...AND WHAT DO I HAVE TO SHOW FOR IT? WHAT DID I ACCOMPLISH?

FEB

...IN THE GREAT SCORECARD FOR HUMAN ENDEAVOR, I JUST LEFT ANOTHER SPACE BLANK...

SAM HURT

HEY, RATLIFF... HAVE YOU HEARD? THEY DECLARED FEBRUARY NULL... IT WON'T COUNT.

REALLY? HEY, THAT'S SWELL!

DAH BAH GOO GAGOO

GOO GAH GOO

DOO BAH GOO GAH!

0   43000 20445

HURT

114

TELL ME A PET PEEVE, RATLIFF.

HERE'S ONE - AFTER ALL THESE YEARS, PEOPLE STILL GO ON AND ON ABOUT HOW THE PRESIDENT IS A THIRD RATE ACTOR FROM OLD B-GRADE MOVIES...

THAT BOTHERS YOU?

I DON'T SEE THE **POINT** OF RELENTLESSLY HARPING ON THE PAST...SO MUCH HAS HAPPENED SINCE HE TOOK OFFICE. I JUST DON'T THINK OF HIM THAT WAY ANYMORE.

WHAT **DO** YOU THINK OF HIM?

HE'S A PRETTY DARN **GOOD** ACTOR!

115

YOU'RE SHOPPING ALONE, WAY AFTER DARK. WITHOUT REALIZING IT, YOU'VE ALREADY CROSSED OVER AN INVISIBLE BOUNDARY INTO A REALM WHERE VALUE AND QUALITY OVERLAP...

—WHERE ALL YOU THOUGHT YOU KNEW ABOUT APPLIANCES IS SWALLOWED UP BY THE IMMENSE SHADOW BEHIND A TINY DOUBT. A SIGNPOST LOOMS UP— YOU'RE IN... "THE BARGAIN ZONE."

WHAT'S WITH **THAT** GUY?

PROBABLY HEARD ONE TOO MANY BAD ROD SERLING IMITATIONS.

*¥⊙!¿ఽⴺⴲ!!

?

SLOW · FAST

117

START WITH TWO INTIMIDATING QUESTIONS. SHAKE SLIGHTLY.

ADD ONE LOOK OF FLABBERGASTED DISBELIEF AND TWO CONFUSING REFERENCES TO PREVIOUS TESTIMONY. MIX WELL.

TOSS IN ONE POINTED GLANCE AT JURY. STRAIN SLOWLY.

I TOLD YOU HE HAD A STYLE WORTH WATCHING.

WITH A GUY LIKE THAT, YOU GOTTA WONDER WHAT GOES ON INSIDE HIS HEAD.

PLACE IN BUTTERED CASSEROLE DISH AND BAKE UNTIL GOLDEN BROWN...

HAVE YOU EVER NOTICED THAT MOST PEOPLE STUMBLE THROUGH LIFE WITHOUT ANY CONTROL OR DIRECTION?

YEAH. ISN'T IT STRANGE.

PERHAPS OUR CULTURE CONDITIONS US TO FOLLOW EACH OTHER AROUND BLINDLY.

THERE'S MORE TO IT THAN THAT.

LIKE WHAT?

WELL, WE'RE SO LOCKED INTO OUR OWN LIMITED PERSPECTIVE THAT WE MISS THE OVERALL PICTURE...

I THINK YOU'RE GETTING TO THE BOTTOM OF IT, RATLIFF.

I'M KNOWN FOR AN OCCASIONAL INSIGHT.

118

HAVE YOU SEEN MY WINDOW?

I **TOLD** YOU I'D KEEP AN EYE OUT!

119

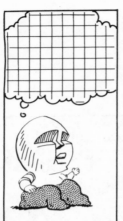

KA·DING
KA·DANG
KLANG

WHAT WAS THAT!?

SOUNDED LIKE A TOASTER OVEN IN A CLOTHES DRYER...

...SO JUST WHEN I THOUGHT I WAS OUT OF THE GARDEN, I'D FIND MYSELF ABOUT TO BUMP INTO THE SAME STATUE OF MYSELF...

WOW!

AND I KNEW SOMEHOW THAT IT WANTED ME TO TOUCH IT. THAT'S WHY I COULDN'T SEEM TO GET AWAY FROM IT.

WHY BOTHER?

BECAUSE IF I TOUCHED IT, I'D BECOME THE STATUE, AND IT WOULD BECOME ME.

SO, WHAT HAPPENED?

WHAT ALWAYS HAPPENS?

THANKS KELLY

120

121

PRESSED AGAINST THE NOON SKY LIKE A CLOUD OR A JET STREAM, I SCAN THE HORIZON...

AS THE EARTH DRIFTS FARTHER BELOW ME, I COME TO SEE IT AS A SLOWLY SHRINKING EGG FROM WHICH I HAVE HATCHED INTO FREEDOM...

IT IS NO LONGER A BURDEN I MUST CARRY ON MY SHOULDERS BUT A STEPPING STONE INTO EXCITING NEW REALMS...

I SEE TINY, ANTLIKE DOTS UPON ITS SURFACE. CAN THEY BE PEOPLE?

MAYBE WE SHOULD COME BACK LATER...

122

UPON MY DEATH I'D LIKE MY WORLDLY GOODS TO BE COLLECTED...

THEN BRING MY FRIENDS AND LOVED ONES THERE, AN LET THEM BE DIRECTED...

THAT EVERY BIT SHALL PASS TO ONE ON WHOM THEY ALL AGREE...

THE CARNAGE THAT RESULTS SHOULD THEN BE SHOWN ON MTV..

AW... THAT'S SWEET...

123

"**E**yebeam ... the best college-generated cartoon since Doonesbury or Bloom County. ... But I think Eyebeam has something neither of those strips has, something simultaneously less trendy and more universal: It has to do with loving your fellow human beings for being fallible. ..."

— **Ed Ward in the *Village Voice***

"Putting originality, inventiveness, and incisiveness aside, Eyebeam is just plain screaming out loud funny."

— **Ben Sargent, editorial cartoonist**

"Eyebeam is, simply, the best unknown strip in America today ... a complex and wonderful group of situations and observations, gentle but telling, and above all completely original."

— ***Austin Chronicle***

"When I see someone reading the strip, I get embarrassed because I'm afraid they'll realize we're related and share some of the same genes."

— **Tom Hurt, brother of author**